5 SECOND ™
Networking

and the law of Association

by **Paul Holland**

Published by SWG Marketing LLC – Little Falls, NJ
PAPERBACK ISBN 978-0-9722059- 0-0

Dedication:

To everyone who isn't there, _yet._

"Genius is 1% inspiration and 99% perspiration"

Thomas Edison

The Challenge

is not coming up with an original thought or idea.

The challenge is having the strength of purpose and will to stand up to conventional thought and say excuse me, I don't think so...

Consider mankind's greatest advancements. Each one began by challenging accepted notions. At one point in time conventional thought was the Sun orbited the Earth, which was of course – flat. It was once commonly believed that disease was transmitted by vapors. People used to say if man were meant to fly he would have been born with wings.

Instead he was born with a mind, the ability to reason, the capability to see beyond what was and to conceive what might be.

Galileo, Copernicus, Pasteur, Hooke, the Wright Brothers, Watt, Newton, Einstein, Fermi, the list could fill this and a thousand books. That is some pretty good company to be numbered with.

We sometimes forget that some of that 99% perspiration Edison referred to can be the product of fear and not just hard work. Fear of the derision of others, being made a mockery of, a "social outcast". Fear of drawing the anger of those who are far more comfortable with accepted notions.

This is in part, my challenge to some accepted notions.

We changed the tools of communication.

They returned the favor *by changing us.*

Napoleon Hill had it and used it fuel his success
but the real secret wasn't "the law of attraction".

Hill called it the Master Mind Principle. The old folks called it "two heads are better than one". It is "The Law of Association". It is not enough to make yourself "attractive to success" you need to live with it, surround yourself with it, eat and breathe it... *AND you need to do that First.*

HERE IS THE PROOF:
Napoleon Hill didn't start out by practicing his principles of success. They hadn't even been written yet. He didn't start out by emanating some mysterious positive force. Hill stated in fact that he didn't think he was the right person to carry Carnegie's message because of "his youth, lack of education and financial resources". In short, Hill was negative on the idea by his own admission. If it was all about attraction, he would have failed, but he had already done something far more important, more basic. He had formed his association with Carnegie, the wealthiest and most powerful man in the world, a self-made man who rose from abject poverty. *First and foremost – we become like those we associate with.*

Most people say they want you to succeed, but in their hearts do they? They will say well-intentioned things like, "I don't want you to be disappointed" or "I don't want you to get hurt" or "Okay, but what's your fall back position?". What they are really saying is, "You belong here in mediocrity with me, where it is safe." That is what they believe. In the course of your association – will they come around to see your vision? Or will you give up your convictions for theirs?

When you look at someone who is successful, what do you feel? Are you happy for them or are you envious, perhaps even bitter? Do you find yourself saying things like, "that should be me" when you could and should be saying, "That will be me".

When you meet success you should say, "Thank you for proving it can be done and please show me the way" and learn by association.

Over the years I have read (and re-read) countless books, taken professional training courses from leading companies, been on the stage as a speaker and listened to a host of others present on numerous topics such as personal development, sales, marketing and more.

The purpose of this book is to boil some of it down for a changing, time compressed, sound byte world (and add a few thoughts of my own).

The way we communicate continues to change radically but we are under an onslaught of information. As a result our need to pool ideas and talents has never been greater.

Success today belongs to people who can compress concepts effectively and recombine them in unique ways. That is why there are no chapters and no page numbers. The book is an exercise in just that. You can pick it up almost anywhere and begin reading for a minute or as long as you like and it will still make sense. It should still deliver value, inspire thought.

It is a collection of quotes, ideas, short essays, anecdotes, predictions, even jokes (what we find amusing is often an amazing window into understanding human nature). You can tell volumes about a culture by what makes them laugh and cry, by who they number among their heroes and villains. Along the way the book explores and explodes a few myths and in the process looks at ways to rethink where our world is going.

The reason why I am writing this now...

In 540 BC Heraclitus said, "The only constant is change".

Today the sum total of human knowledge doubles every 18 years and the pace is accelerating. It is not merely change but the rate of change that is so unsettling because we can never seem to find any steady ground.

BUT THERE IS GOOD NEWS!

First, without change (by definition) opportunity cannot exist. In fact the status quo is the mortal enemy of opportunity. Faster change just means there are more possibilities, more often... but in the immortal words of Douglas MacArthur, "Chance favors the prepared man." One of the purposes of this little book is to help you prepare yourself to take full advantage of what is coming.

The second bit of good news is that <u>Heraclitus was wrong</u>. There is one great constant to which we can anchor... our own human nature. Since before we daubed paint on cave walls man has hoped, loved, feared, envied, dreamed... that basic makeup has never changed.

It is through an understanding of our own nature (and that of those around us) that we can learn to adapt and in the process put ourselves in the best possible position to succeed.

Tapping into that common thread which joins us puts the power of the Law of Association into play and 5 Second Networking is the first best tool to fast track it.

Welcome.

5 Second Networking is more than just a means of connecting with other people in a meeting.

It is a practical method for communicating complete ideas effectively in the absence of time while competing against the avalanche of information overload.

We changed the tools of communication and in return they changed us. This is a way of clarifying thought and concentrating focus based on that knowledge. It can be used with regard to virtually any aspect of goal setting and it consists of five steps:

1. DEFINE – What is it you are looking to achieve? Write it down.

2. POWER WORDS – Cross out all of the extraneous language, leaving only the "power words" behind.

3. IDENTIFY THE CORE VALUE – What is the single most important aspect, the benefit that these convey from the standpoint of the person you are telling it to?

4. CONDENSE & CLARIFY – Using these words, construct a concise, memorable position statement.

5. PRACTISE, PRACTISE, PRACTISE – You should be able to deliver your statement in under 5 seconds.

This exercise in 5 Second Networking is your first best means to create a powerful and memorable message, whether you are attempting to explain what your business does, what your most profitable customer looks like or what you are seeking next in your business…

The best way to combat information overload and shrinking attention spans is to pack maximum power into tiny armor piecing packages. They become mental billboards, pre-qualifying and attracting interest because they are so focused.

5 Second Networking has additional values.

The process itself is a mental discipline that causes the participant to continually challenge and sharpen their own vision using the metrics of their customers, prospects, partners and potential stakeholders as a standard. It helps you better understand your own business.

Fear of speaking in public is the most common of all phobias. 5 Second Networking minimizes that aspect of a meeting thereby encouraging participation from people who would traditionally avoid such venues. It broadens the pool.

Since people know their "pitch" buy rote, they can focus more attention on others and the opportunity they may represent. Elevator pitches are really sales pitches. While they are going on, the majority of attention is on selling not buying. That is not a productive scenario. 5 second Networking is not about selling. It is about creating a single, powerful impression. It is about linking what you do most profitably and with what you need most next in your business with your name in the mind of the others there. That has far greater lasting value. 5 Second Networking also frees up time. Assume that it takes an average of 2 ½ minutes for each person at a meeting to give their elevator speech, it would take an hour for 24 people. How many will be truly memorable? Assume it only took 10 seconds on average for each person. Now the room is alive with energy and active networking is able to go on after only 4 MINUTES! This also facilitates much larger meetings in manageable time frames.

We asked technology for time instead it gave us speed…

and we have confused the two.

That is why we always feel a half step behind, why we experience things like road rage when we feel we have been delayed a few seconds in our daily headlong rush.

How often in the course of your day do you feel pressured by a sense of urgency, the need to "do it now"?   One of the most popular tricks in advertising is the concept behind a "one day sale". If you don't do it immediately the opportunity will vanish – forever! Hogwash.

What companies have managed to do with all of these "special sales" is to train people NOT to buy. They know the next sale is coming next week, next month… Unless they have a burning need they will wait until they see exactly what they want at a price they are willing to pay.

It has also managed to do something else.

It has blinded us to opportunity because everything we see and hear is yet another "Quantum Leap". What is truly amazing just how tiny a quantum leap can be.   It has been demonstrated that repeated exposure to violence in the media has caused people to become desensitized to it. As a result movies, video games, music et al become increasingly violent, people become more calloused, voila – death spiral.

The same thing happens with technology and the opportunities it spawns – "what are you going to do to wow me now?"

Successful people train themselves to see beyond the veil of clutter.

In the information age
Google didn't become
a multi-billion company
almost overnight
by creating information...

They did it helping people find it.
Google doesn't mine information –
They enable it for those who do
by supplying the picks and shovels ...

Creating your own
Strategic Network Alliances
establishing yourself as a nexus
linking people and resources
allows you to become
your own "search engine"
that is empowerment...

Whether you call it the Law of Association, the
Master Mind principle or just sound reasoning – it
forms the foundation of success.

The purpose of a great leader, mentor or teacher -

is to convey knowledge,

inspire thought,

cultivate wisdom,

empower people

and in the process

make themselves obsolete!

Children's stories are fascinating…

Take for example the story of the **Little Red Hen**.

She finds some wheat and despite her best efforts she cannot successfully enlist the assistance of the other various animals to help in doing all the sundry tasks of planting, harvesting, grinding flour, baking etc.

In fact the only time she gets a rousing chorus of "YES" from her barnyard companions is when she asks the final question of; "Who would like to help me eat the bread?" (By the way, she does this only to rub their noses in the fact that she was right and they were wrong. How many of the animals do you think might resent that for a very long time?) The Little Red Hen has industry and initiative down pat but she needs to work on her people skills (especially graciousness).

If she truly wanted help, the Little Red Hen's mistake was in not asking the last question first. It was in not getting the others to buy into her vision, for example; "Would you like to eat some nice, hot bread fresh out of the oven? Good, then pick up a hoe."

The path to success shortens and obstacles shrink when "my" vision becomes "our" vision.

Jack sees John searching around on the ground and he goes up to him and asks, "Did you lose something?"

John says, "Yes, I lost my keys."

Jack helped him look unsuccessfully for a while and asked, "Are you sure this is where you had them last?"

John pointed and replied, "No, I had them over there."

Jack shook his head and asked, "Then why aren't you looking over there?"

John replied, "Well, the light is better here..."

***

In business and in life, how often do we avoid difficult or unpleasant tasks by working peripherally around the problem instead of confronting the heart of the matter directly, head-on?

Other than cheese and wine – not much improves with age. Cut straight to the chase so that issues can be resolved quickly and put behind you - OR - you can simply prolong them. How often do we come up with excuses no matter how absurd to rationalize aberrant behavior?

Procrastination wastes opportunity by devouring our most precious resource, time.

Failure

isn't good or bad.

It is just necessary.

~

What is *NOT* necessary is repeating failure. Not learning from our mistakes is the path that makes failure into a habit… and that *is* bad, very bad.

So why do we continue the same behavior that has already shown itself as unsuccessful?

- We refuse to Un-Learn.
- We can be reluctant to discard old notions, theories and preconceptions even after they are proven wrong or harmful.
- We are driven by bad habits formed over time.
- Our competitive nature considers the admission of a mistake as a weakness. As a result we cannot admit to having been wrong.

In reality – the inability to admit a mistake is the ultimate weakness.
(because we learn nothing)

To Succeed – become "UN" principled

1. Un-Learn – the ability to shed mental and emotional baggage. The landscape changes too fast to hang onto out-dated misconceptions. Principles and values are timeless – but ideas and notions have expiration dates. Throw them out.

2. Unafraid – either you master fear, or it masters you. Those are the only two choices

3. Undiluted – goals should always be served FULL STRENGTH, don't settle for less.

4. Uncluttered – no matter what you need next in obtaining your goal always be as specific as possible.

5. Undivided – once you have set your sights on a goal, never look away. If it is worth having it requires your undivided attention.

6. Undeterred – people who do not share your vision (particularly well intentioned people) will try to dissuade you in your course. Thank them. Consider their feed back and do what you need to do.

7. Unfinished – the road to success is never finished. In the pursuit of excellence, you can never sit on your laurels.

Predictions are based principally on two factors
– Human Nature & Economic Necessity –
these are merely logical projections based on known conditions

The Cultural Evolution

The Internet and such phenomena as Social Networking will erase traditionally imposed political boundaries in lieu of virtually imposed cultural ones. These groups will be elective based on jointly held beliefs, language, history and other cultural markers.

Look at the example of the fall of the old Soviet Union. Despite having been co-joined under the USSR, countries immediately divided back along ancient cultural guidelines.

Look at the difficulties arising in areas such as sub-Saharan Africa where political boundaries have grouped or separated people artificially. The recombining of North and South Vietnam or the separation of India and Pakistan – people want to and will establish their own boundaries separate and apart from those imposed by outside mapmakers.

The Internet is the great facilitator of this because it recognizes no pre-existing boundaries. It is already happening and accelerating. Immigration and travel have set the stage. There are currently more ex-patriot Irish than there are people living in Ireland. It is only natural to see the rise of a virtual Latin world, a virtual Southeast Asian world, a Roman Catholic world... the point is that all of these and thousands more are possible and natural outcomes. The trick to universal success is to encourage cooperation rather than competition through points of intersection and overlap.

The practice of making predictions helps to clarify thought.

The teacher said, "Give me a sentence with an object."

The student replied, "You look very lovely today teacher."

Then the teacher asked, "And what is the object of the sentence?"

The student replied, "Better grades."

***

We are all subject to the same faults and failings. It is an integral part of who and what we are. It is unavoidable, however it is also predictable. There are always those who will seek to use our baser instincts to their advantage.

Since we are governed by human nature we should exercise great care in "electing" that government by choosing our friends and advisors wisely; by weighing their counsel and everyone's motives (including our own).

Be careful – we become like those we associate with.

Children's stories are fascinating…

Remember the story of **The Ugly Duckling**.

All the other ducklings bullied this creature unmercifully, just because he looked different. Surprise – he was different. He was a cygnet.

You might think the point of the story was to be careful who you pick on – because every dog has his day, but I don't like that idea. It implies that being a bully is okay as long as it can't backfire on you.

There are more (and more interesting) levels to this story, particularly relevant to today.

First, in order to change his circumstance he had to be transformed. Simply becoming a large ugly duck wasn't going to make it. It reinforces the concept of – if you want something to change in your life, then you need to change something in your life.

Second, bullying has always been a problem and now with the advent of a handheld Internet, cyber bullying is epidemic. You now no longer have to be the biggest or the strongest. You don't have to risk a black eye or a bloody nose. You can remotely and anonymously shred an opponent psychologically. Isn't technology grand?

Technology enables us to do things both good and bad because it possesses power without conscience. Our job, like the ugly duckling, is to grow up and evolve before our baser natures do us all in.

The "Law of Attraction" and the "Law of Distraction"

Napoleon Hill wrote his self help classic "Think and Grow Rich" in 1937. It was re-purposed in the popular book and movie "The Secret" recently.

Hill's volume of work set forth systematic programs for self improvement based on sound principles of human nature. It was in a word; masterful in that it identified practical traits, tips and techniques to help people take charge of their lives and emulate the behavior of successful people.

Hill espoused "the law of attraction" and there are many who believe it is an immutable force – there are many who dismiss it. Whether you subscribe to it or not, one aspect that does hold up is "like values attract". Honest people want to surround themselves with others who value honesty. Industrious people gravitate to other industrious people and so on. <u>We value in others what we value in ourselves</u>. That is simply logical.

Ultimately, the empowered individual assumes personal responsibility for their decisions and direction. Regardless of the source, they become their own force through their decisions and actions. They know that better, more self-aware choices on average create better outcomes.

Where the concept of the law of attraction as an irresistible force does fall down is that the world can play by other rules such as favoritism, nepotism, bias and bigotry that have the ability to trump it. You might be the most positive, productive person in a company only to find yourself replaced by the boss's nephew.

What makes the "law of attraction" work - is the work you are willing to do because you believe in it. What makes the "law of attraction" work is the law of distraction. By believing that we cannot fail supported by this unseen power we look beyond the work, the sacrifice and the effort. We see problems as mere momentary challenges and opportunities because we are goal oriented. In a culture where deferred gratification has gone the way of the tyrannosaur – patience, long-term planning, and staying power help give you an edge over the vast majority. People may argue that "The law of attraction" isn't physics but rather a belief system. Regardless, it simply does not recognize failure as an option. The result is that there are the only two permissible outcomes; to achieve your goal or to continue working toward it. At the end of the day however, whether you assign it to physics or belief - it our focus, effort, attitude and energy that will bring about success just as the lack of it will relegate us to mediocrity.

A magician goes to the booking agent and says, "I have a great new closer for my act. Get this... I saw a woman in half!"

The agent looks at him and says, "Are you crazy? That's not new... That's one of the oldest tricks in the book."

The magician smiled and said, *"LENGTHWISE?"*

***

Never be afraid to apply new solutions to old problems. The old adage of "if it ain't broke – don't fix it" doesn't hold in an evolving and changing world. Often changing times bring new methods, materials and tools. Doing something in a particular way may have been profitable once but it may no longer be and vice versa. We need to acquire the ability to "unlearn".

Most "creative solutions" are not ground breaking, they are merely adaptive. They come about simply by looking at new combinations of what has been applied elsewhere.

Consider this analogy; Adaptive Creativity is like finding a new use for a screwdriver. Original Creativity would be inventing the screwdriver. There are many more adaptive solutions than original ones.

In a world of change, Adaptive and Original Creativity are some of the most important skills you can and should develop. Most people see "the problem". Successful people see an opportunity disguised as a problem. Problem solving is really about brushing the obstacles away to get at the opportunity.

We can only learn from experience.

It can be our own experience,

or that of someone else.

Both work.

One hurts less...

One of my personal ambitions is to be the second person through the minefield...

One of the fastest and most efficient ways to solve problems is to bring more diverse resources to bear on it. That means more people and diverse points of view. That concentrates the broadest array of experience possible to help optimize your outcome.

A physicist walks into a diner and says to the waitress, "I'd like to order chaos…"

***

A Zen master walks up to a hotdog cart and says, "Make me one with everything…"

***

The relevance of all this is "relevance".
To be successful, you have to be a good communicator or your dreams, your goals, your ideas, your vision will remain forever that – yours, exclusively.

Communication requires four parts, the sender, the message, the medium and the receiver. If your target audience doesn't get it because the message or the medium doesn't have relevance to them – you can waste your breath all day long and it won't make a difference.

You can practice and hone your speaking and presentation skills but you will never become a truly accomplished speaker until you are an even better listener. That is what keeps you relevant. Improvement can only really be achieved with objective feedback. That's how you will know that your vision has become our vision, that the receiver has bought in and made it their own.

"I had to succeed, because I finally ran out of things that didn't work." Thomas Edison

SUCCESS

is not the
Absence of Failure

***

it is the
Absence of Quitting

our actions are not driven by emotions...

our reactions are.

When you surrender yourself to an emotion such as anger or love, you are giving away control over yourself.

For example; if another person does something and as a result you become angry – you are permitting their action to catalyze and determine your reaction, your anger. You have given them control over your emotional state.

Control of our emotions does NOT mean we are emotionless. It means that we have the ability to channel what we feel, tempered by reason and logic to serve us.

Our emotional being, what makes us passionate about things is like a steam boiler at full pressure. Reason constitutes the pipes, valves and turbines that can take that stored up power and put it where it will serve us best. Regardless of who may stoke the fire – it is reason that permits us to reap the benefit.

The bottom line is *someone WILL control your emotions*. The question is; will it be you?

The Myth of SUCCESS and FAILURE

A big part of the myth derives from the fact that we permit others to tell us what success and failure look like but it is different for all of us.

Based exclusively on "monetary worth" someone like Mahatma Gandhi, Albert Schweitzer or Mother Theresa would be dismal failures but I can't imagine too many people who would ever think of them in that way. They simply measured success with a different yardstick.

The more interesting concept is that old imposter, *FAILURE*.

Consider for a moment if we define failure as "the state of not having achieved success" – we need only add one word to radically alter its nature. The definition should correctly read as, "the state of not having achieved success, yet." That addition now means that failure is the road to success and isn't that the reality of it?

From that perspective, you cannot fail unless you depart from the path to success – we must choose to fail.

Too often we hit obstacles and let them stop our progress because we make the mistake of thinking we've failed. But that is not true unless you want to.

REMEMBER:

Always treat failure as an event.

Always treat success as a process.

By doing that failure becomes finite with a beginning and an end, but success becomes a way of life.

The Only Thing More Infectious Than *ENTHUSIASM*

is the lack of it!

Points of intersection…

In examining the myriad volumes on subjects such as self-improvement, sales, marketing, biographies of successful people… certain common threads always emerge. There are shared qualities and characteristics which can be boiled down and condensed to the following:

1. **Vision.** Successful people have a clear image of what success looks like. If you cannot focus on a result; you cannot craft a pathway to it. Often, what we may think of as our goal is misleading. For example; you might say, I want to earn a million dollars a year – but what you want is not really the money. You want what that amount of money might enable.

2. **Dedication.** You can call it self-sacrifice, strength of purpose, focus, commitment… Nothing comes without a price. It is ironic that often people who complain the loudest that life isn't *fair* because they have to walk are the same ones who refuse to pay the *fare* to ride.

3. **Self-Awareness.** You need to be aware of where you are now, your strengths and weaknesses. You have to willing to be brutally honest with yourself and to accept feedback, even when it is unpleasant. To map a straight course requires both a beginning and an end. To stay on that course requires feedback.

4. **Development.** One reason why you are not where you want to be *YET* is that things are missing. Your success is dependant in part on paying the price to acquire these things. Get comfortable with the idea that development is not an event, it is a never-ending process. How could it be static in a world that is constantly changing and evolving? This process can be divided into two areas:
   a. **Personal development.** These things like include: education, visualization, ethics, creative thinking and problem-solving… these are the kind of things you do to improve you.

b. ***Interpersonal development.*** You must deal with other people, so you need things like: team building, communication skills, mentoring, leadership, effective listening, and empathy... the kinds of things that affect how you interact with others.

5. ***Reassessment.*** We do not exist in a vacuum and we cannot control all things *BUT* we can control how we react to and assimilate them. Constant learning and feedback are keys to maintaining us on track to our goals.

6. ***Attitude.*** Virtually any skill can be acquired and honed through repetition. You can program a robot to paint like Da Vinci but it cannot appreciate the art. Attitudes can only be acquired on a visceral level through an emotional attachment. I can borrow skills from other peoples. I can rent assets from other people. That is not true of attitude. Attitude can only be cultivated. It grows within from the seeds planted by others and we in turn sow the seeds of our attitude in others, our families, friends and co-workers. Like any successful garden, our attitude requires constant weeding, nurture and care.

BOTTOM LINE:
If you want better outcomes – cultivate those habits which make you a better person.

The better able you are to deal with people, the greater your likelihood of success.

Find ways for everyone to win and success will seek you out.

most endure change
(they see it as a hardship)

some react to change
(they see it as a necessary evil)

truly successful people
~ become ~
agents of change...
(and create their own opportunity in the process)

A snake thinks everything thinks like a snake.

A dog thinks everything thinks like a dog.

The reason is because that is their only frame of reference. It is all they know. The majority cannot fathom how successful people "do it" because they don't think that way. They are mired in self doubt, anxiety, anger, self pity... successful people don't waste time and energy on such activities. Under-performing people can't imagine not dwelling on such things.

Take it a step further –

Dishonest and unethical people rationalize their behavior by thinking they will "get the other guy before he gets me". Theirs' is the law of the cannibal – eat or be eaten. (The problem with that of course is that no matter what you do; sooner or later it is your turn in the pot.)

Conversely people who are honest, industrious, loyal, trustworthy, team players expect those around them to respond in kind. Because they think that way they assume everyone else does as well. The challenge of course is when good people run into the other variety. For some unfortunate reason it always seems that bad habits and attitudes are more infectious than good ones...
(So be careful out there.)

It is only natural that we seek out those with whom we share a common bond, a compatible set of values. It is because we understand and appreciate each other.

Ask yourself; what kind of people would you like to be surrounded by?

Choose. Then take action to cultivate and exhibit those traits in yourself that you want to see in people around you. Then when you find them, hang on!

TECHNOLOGY

causes
the value of what we know
to diminish

&

the value of how well
we adapt
to increase

Moral: What we learn pales in significance
to *how* we learn.

Children's stories are fascinating...

Take the story of **The Ant and the Grasshopper** -

The grasshopper plays all day while his friend the ant labors to store up supplies for the winter... The outcome is predictable.

The grasshopper isn't "bad" – merely foolish, out only for himself. The ant is a fully vested member of a community. It is the competitive and cooperative models juxtaposed.

Let's take it to a deeper level. One of the classic questions in theology is - "Why do bad things happen to good people." You might also ask the inverse, "Why do bad people profit at the expense of good people?"

I notice that nobody asks why good things happen to good people or gets upset when a "bad person" encounters misfortune.

The bottom line is: *THINGS HAPPEN TO PEOPLE.*

What happens to us and to the people we are connected to occurs because of the decisions we make, the actions we take and fail to take.

Are we influenced by forces that exist beyond our control? YES.

However it begs the question, are these forces beyond our control because they are beyond our capability to influence or is it because of our failure to plan and act? For example, I cannot control the weather – but I can buy an umbrella.

We live in an age when many people feel they are "Entitled". An empowered person recognizes that the only thing we are entitled to is to make our own decisions and in conjunction with that, that we are responsible for the outcome of those decisions.

The Law Of Association

Napoleon Hill referred to his master mind principle, building alliances to tap into the resources of others. The law of Association goes beyond that and consists of three points:
1. Things that are alike attract one another
2. We become more like that which we associate with
3. Over time 1 & 2 create a cycle of reinforcement and refinement

How many times have we heard the old adage, "One bad apple spoils the barrel"? We worry about our kids "running with the wrong crowd". We say things like, "It isn't what you know – it's who you know."

Your success if fueled by the establishment and maintenance of a Strategic Network of Alliances.

YOU ARE EITHER NETWORKING – or – YOU ARE NOT WORKING!

The two classic mistakes in the creation of building a truly effective Strategic Network of Alliances are:

First, we network exclusively within our comfort zone. Bankers only talk to bankers, engineers talk to other engineers... _Likes Attract_ but WHERE IS THE FRESH EXCHANGE OF INFORMATION? Further, we stay within our socio-economic strata. If I want to become a person of high net worth, don't I need to associate with those kinds of people too? How else will we learn from them? BREAK DOWN THE BARRIERS. No one will do it for you. Get comfortable with being uncomfortable.

Second, a true strategic alliance is never unilateral. It must be based on mutual benefit – in the principles of cooperation. Both parties must profit. You are probably thinking; WAIT A MINUTE – If I want to associate with successful, high net worth individuals what could I have that they would want? A very natural question best answered by the relationship between Hill and Carnegie. On the surface they were polar opposites, the "Steel King" and the "kid" but only if you measured them with the same yardstick. Hill sought fame and fortune. Carnegie had that to burn. What Carnegie wanted was an empty vessel to fill with the legacy of his philosophy of success. He could not have given that to one of his millionaire friends could he? They wouldn't take it without interjecting their own philosophies.. It was the disparity of their stations in life that made the match.

How do you bridge the chasm to begin such an association?

Two things:

First, stand out from the crowd by becoming a person of interest. Read, study, and develop successful habits such as industry, acuity, insight, vision, focus, industry, interpersonal skills... The more you do along these lines the further you will remove yourself from the masses. Sadly most people fear power including their own greatness. Instead they choose to remain cloaked in obscurity. These are two of nature's most common defenses – camouflage and the safety of the herd.

Most people fear appearing on the radar of powerful people. Successful minds covet that position.

Second, fish where the fish are. Organizations, associations, seminars, meetings... *It is NOT about stalking people*, which will only lead you into trouble. The best way to make someone run away is to chase them. It is simply about positioning yourself to win. When you do that, when you display the qualities that make you attractive - others will choose you.

If you wish to become noticed – make yourself into someone worthy of note and don't hide your light under a basket. Become proficient in the art of Empowered Asking.

An elderly couple, killed in an accident, found themselves being given a tour of heaven by Saint Peter. "Here is your ocean side estate; over there are the tennis courts, swimming pool, and two golf courses. If you need any anything at all, just stop by any of the many shops located throughout the area and ask. They will give you anything you need."

The old man hissed at his wife after Saint Peter walked off, "We could have been here ten years ago if you hadn't listened to all that stupid advice about oat bran, exercise, and low-fat diets!"

***

We can debate the relative merits of society and its values, but deferred gratification has gone the way of the dodo, hind sight is always perfect and there is always someone to blame other than ourselves.

The first step in seizing control of and shaping your future is to recognize two things – you are responsible for the choices you make (including the choice to "surrender" our autonomy to someone else) and all things come with a price that must be paid.

When you make the conscious decision to accept these facts – you are on the road to personal empowerment.

Nobody is trying to replace you Frank, that's crazy talk...

One man's crazy – is another man's reality.

There are some things you should never sneer at like:

another person's dreams, beliefs, fears or troubles...

but that doesn't mean that you _have_ to participate in them.

*All these things and more were considered **IMPOSSIBLE:***

Circumnavigating the world
Heavier than air flight
Running a four minute mile
Breaking the sound barrier
Television
Splitting the atom
Open heart surgery
Space travel
Radio transmission & reception
Artificial heart
Flying non-stop from New York to Paris
Submarine travel
Electric lights
Steam engine
Panama canal
Telephones
Cloning
Lasers
Audio recording
Internal combustion engine
Refrigeration
Radar
GPS
Computer
The Internet

everything

is

impossible

until somebody does it...

Do you hate your job? ...or something else in your life?

Pick the reason why:

My job is miserable	☐
I am miserable	☐
All of the above	☐

In physics there is something called the Observer Effect, which basically states that in the process of observing something we alter the conditions of the experiment. A classic example of this would be checking the air pressure in a car tire with a hand held gauge. As we check the pressure a tiny amount of air is released from the tire. In measuring it – we change it.

If you think your job makes you miserable, it is pretty hard to be an objective observer of conditions. (You already think it is rotten.)

It is human nature once we have formed an opinion we look for things that support that position and not for things that refute it.

Rather than saying you don't like your job, tell me why – specifically. Is there anything you do like about your job (after all you took the position, you stay there – there must be something)?

"Things" don't make us miserable. We do that to ourselves. We choose our circumstances based on a weighted set of preferences. For example: You are considering two jobs. One pays less now but has more upward mobility. You decide which matters more but if you choose the "pays less now" option, why would you complain about the pay? You should be focused on the advancement track you signed on for and grumbling about the check at the end of the month won't help that very much, will it?

A negative attitude could cost you both pay and advancement, but that is you – not the job.

The fastest road
to unhappiness is
counting the
fortunes
of others.

The success or failure of others does not preclude or guarantee my outcome.

But wasting time and energy focusing on the fortunes of others drains those resources from my own efforts and limits my own opportunity for success.

> *Think and Grow Rich* – *first published in 1937*
>
> *How to Win Friends and Influence People* – *first published in 1937*
>
> *The Power of Positive Thinking* – *first published in 1952*

When people like Napoleon Hill, Dale Carnegie and Norman Vincent Peale were writing the American people and their economy were a radically different landscape.

In 1937 we were in the midst of the Great Depression. In 1952 we were in the boom of the Eisenhower years. People believed that you went to work for a company and stayed until they gave you a gold watch and you left to go fishing.

Opportunities for women in the workplace were negligible and most of those only came as a result of WWII. Segregation was commonplace. Polio was killing and crippling over 60,000 a year in the US in 1952.

In 1950 only about 7% of Americans had a college education and only another 30% of the population had a high school diploma.

In 1937, there was only one telephone for every 15 people in the US.

I could go on and on but the important point is this:

Technology changes... Human nature doesn't.

That is why these books and countless spin-offs continue to be relevant and are sold today.

If I knew everything there is to know about cellular telephone technology today - all of it could be obsolete in 3 to 5 years.

If you understand your own motivations and those of people around you - it will still be valid decade after decade.

A police officer in a small town stopped a motorist who was speeding down Main Street. "But officer," the man began, "I can explain."

"Just be quiet," snapped the officer. "Or I'm going to let you cool your heels in jail until the chief gets back."

"But, officer, I just wanted to say,..."

"I told you to keep quiet! Now you're going to jail!"

A few hours later the officer looked in on his prisoner and said, "Lucky for you that the chief's at his daughter's wedding. At least he should be in a good mood when he gets back."

"Don't count on it," answered the fellow in the cell. "I'm the groom."

***

What makes this relevant is that human nature loves to see "the mighty" topple. (Especially when we think they abuse their authority.) We think that humbling our boss, our leaders, or others of importance in some way elevates "us". It doesn't. It simply provides the illusion that their position was unearned, that they "are no better than we are..."

Truly empowered people recognize that fall of others does not make us rise. If anything, seeing others fall only makes us more content to stay where we are.

The Myth of Technological Growth

People think the growth of technology looks like this.

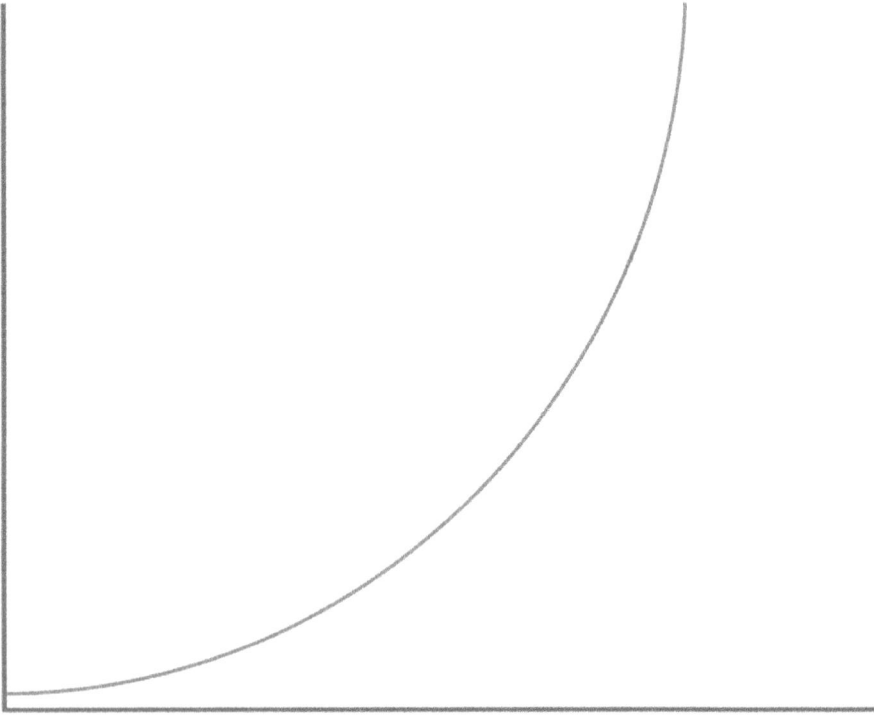

That it simply expands geometrically -

but that is not really what happens…

Technology actually grows more like this, in stops and starts.

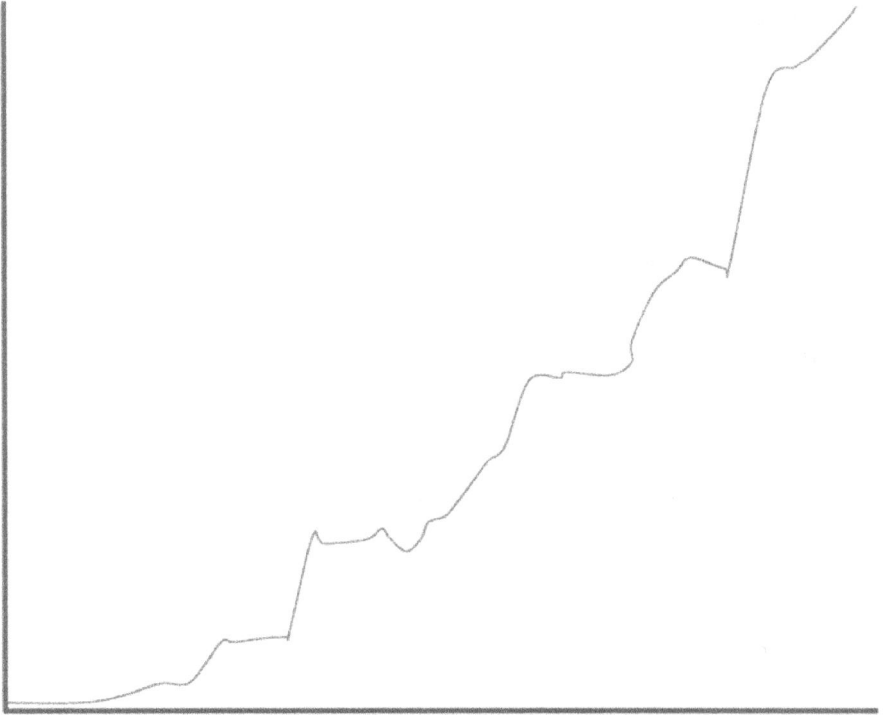

It is increasing at a dramatic rate but it makes mistakes, hits bottlenecks and not every discovery or advancement carries the same importance. Consequently the upward curve is populated by peaks, valleys and plateaus. That is GREAT news. A smooth curve it would mean that if you were not in on the "big breakthrough" you missed out. Opportunity would quickly diminish BUT the reality is that new possibilities abound every time the line changes direction regardless of the direction.

To truly appreciate the power of a technology, never look at what it does. Seek to understand what it enables because in the tangent possibilities that radiate from that point reside countless opportunities.

For example: The value of Bessemer's converter wasn't the ability to mass produce steel – it was the availability of virtually unlimited quantities of affordable steel that yanked a bottleneck and changed the world.

Children's stories are fascinating...

Remember the story of **The Boy Who Cried Wolf**.

He was asked to keep guard over a flock of sheep in the night and because it was about as exciting as watching paint dry or grass grow, he thought he would have a little fun by crying "WOLF".

Needless to say the villagers came running only to find the young man having a good laugh at their expense. To put it mildly, they were less than amused.

As the night wore on, the boy did it again (he was not a fast learner) and the villagers, after chastising the shepherd soundly returned to their beds.

Naturally after they had gone, a wolf did show up and feasted on the sheep as the helpless young man tried desperately to get anyone to pay attention to him. Having already been fooled more than once – they ignored him.

Consider how this relates to our lives today.

Let's start at the end. In ignoring the boy, the villagers actually wind up punishing themselves! They are the ones who lost the sheep. How often out of a sense of spite and revenge do we harbor anger and resentment? In the process we poison ourselves. The people who injured you don't care if you are resentful (if they intended to hurt you the fact that you continue to boil would make them happy if anything).

The villagers are angry at the boy *BUT THEY LEFT HIM THERE.* When he demonstrated he couldn't be trusted, they should have fired him and put someone else in his place. The first time I can blame the kid, but not the second or third time. That is the big take away from this story. Someone may hurt you once (whether intentionally or unintentionally) – but we choose whether to multiply that hurt by holding onto it or to cut it off cleanly and be done. Make injuries, failure, pain just an event – learn from them and let them end. Then they become stepping stones in the path to success, which is a process.

A little old lady applied for a visa with US immigration.

In reading down the list of questions, the official asked, "Do you advocate the overthrow of the government by violence or subversion?"

She thought a second and replied, "Gosh, if those are my only choices - violence, I guess."

***

Limiting choices limits outcomes. Sadly that limitation is usually self-imposed.

People tend to go where they are lead, whether or not they truly believe in what they are doing or even if it is in their best interest.

As leaders we have an obligation to choose our paths carefully.

One of the side effects of technology is "Instant Information".
Simply because we can grasp a piece of data quickly does not mean that it is complete, accurate or relevant but we are often tempted to act or answer just as quickly anyway. An empowered individual avoids rash and impulsive action simply because it is expedient.

Beware – the instant gratification society encourages rash behavior.

**One of the worst things
you can give a person is a diploma...**

it implies they are done learning...

Attitude can only be cultivated.

It grows within us
from the seeds we permit
to be planted by others
and we in turn sow the seeds of our attitude
in our families, friends and co-workers.

Like any successful garden,
our attitudes requires constant
weeding, nurture and care.

Examine your attitude
and ask yourself -
What can I hope to harvest,
From what is planted here?

Empowered Asking

Most people view the act of asking for things as a sign of weakness. Actually – it all depends on how you are asking.

When we feel we do not actually have the right to ask for whatever it is. It is "unearned" – we are in essence begging, not asking.

At the other extreme, some people will demand things based on some sense of entitlement either real or imagined.

Either way – this is not <u>Empowered Asking</u>.

Consider the act of asking your boss for a raise, simply because you want more money or you have been with the company a long time.

You may feel that you are undeserving and "beg" or you may feel that you are entitled and "demand". In either case you decrease your opportunity for success because neither position is supported.

In the case of Empowered Asking, you might approach your boss by citing how you have been tasked with and are handling functions outside of your previous job description. You have assumed greater responsibility, brought more business into the company, you have demonstrated your greater worth...

You begin Empowered Asking by creating a case for your cause – a position of strength. You are now standing on more of a peer to peer level. It is no longer just the "Boss" and his "Employee" – it is two successful mindsets discussing value and mutual benefit.

This could be a salesperson looking for the order; a student seeking to enlist a mentor... what matters is creating an empowered position from which to ask.

When we ask the right questions of the right people, at the right time – we get the right answer.

So what are the:

RIGHT QUESTIONS - Understand exactly what you need and ask for it specifically and precisely. Do not deviate. If you need to raise money in your business for example, *How Much, For What Purpose, What Outcome Will That Create, When Will There Be A Return???*
Right Questions come from Empowered Asking. If my position and my request are cloudy, even if I am asking the Right Person at the Right Time, the potential for a successful outcome is dramatically reduced.

RIGHT PEOPLE - If you are asking someone for something that is far beyond their ability to give, you are wasting their time and yours. HOWEVER, if you are functioning in a cooperative model, where people have formed true Strategic Networking Alliances you are not asking just one person, you are telescoping into their associations. While they personally may not be able to supply you with the resources you need, others within their circle of influence may be able to do just that. That is why a cooperative business model is so much more powerful than a competitive one. Within it, the Law of Association increases geometrically in power.

RIGHT TIME – In sales there is a rule. Yes means Yes. No means, not yet. There are reasons why the time may not yet be right. The person asking may ask before they are ready for the answer they seek – they are not asking in an empowered fashion. The person being asked may not have the resources, or not be focused on the question or its outcome. They cannot "see" you because they are looking at something else.

For the outcomes we want, we must work to align all three.

Predictions are based principally on two factors
– Human Nature & Economic Necessity –
these are merely logical projections based on known conditions

Education

Education will continue to shift from "fact based" to "skills based".
The proliferation of technology and the broadening of the knowledge base causes "facts" to lose relevancy and/or become obsolete. What is more important in a rapidly changing world is the skill to access the "facts" and determine their relevancy. Skill sets will fall into three categories, core, secondary and peripheral. A core skill would be an enabling capability such as reading or math. An example of a secondary skill would be a particular field such as accounting. A peripheral skill would be knowledge specific such a version of QuickBooks.

Peripheral skills will change and evolve constantly. Secondary skills will morph more slowly over time. Core competency will change little if at all. Because of economic considerations in terms of utility and available resources – primary education will retreat to basic core skill sets just as peripheral skills will move farther out the chain..

A college education today can easily top $100,000 and the most common major of incoming freshmen is "undecided". Such a system cannot sustain economically. More young people will be looking to alternative educational pathways. Apprenticeships, interning, trade schools, and work experience – again opportunities will abound in this time of change by proving young people with these alternative pathways and people of every age with tools to improve their skills.

In this evolving world the two most important aspects of education will be to learn how to learn and to learn how to un-learn.

Children's stories are fascinating…

How about **The Emperor's New Clothes**.

You recall the story, about a vain and foolish Emperor who gets conned by two men. They pretend to make him a "magical" suit of magnificent clothes that cannot be seen by anyone who is foolish.

There is no suit of clothes.
But no one can say so without risking ridicule.

Of course at the end while parading through the city stark naked, a child in his innocence cries out the truth and the plot of the two schemers is exposed. (Sorry maybe a poor choice of words.)

How often do we permit our vision to be obscured by others telling us what we want to hear instead of what we need to know?

How often do we permit "groupthink" to seize control of a situation?

How often do we impose our vision on others rather than have others buy in and partner with us because they really believe in it?

How often is that lone voice of dissent ignored or dismissed unwisely? If someone is willing to risk the wrath of the group – they must really believe in what they are saying… maybe there is something there.

THE 5 SECOND NETWORKING PITCH

If you time people at a networking meeting when they deliver their "elevator pitch" you will find they often get a little nervous and ramble on and on.

That is the *WORST* thing you can do.

1. Others want their "Moment in the Sun" and the longer you go on – the more you are preventing that (very negative impression). It is just human nature.

2. The longer you are speaking, the greater the likelihood you will say something that will turn the listening audience "off". For example, you might mention something about an IRA account. A listener thinks, "Oh I don't need that" and click they erase your entire message.

3. No one can be all things to all people. The more you try to "cram" into your message the more you will sound like everyone else and the less you will sound like YOU.

4. Speaking in public is the most common of all phobias. As a rule the, the longer you speak the greater the opportunity to make a mistake, forget something or repeat yourself.

The concept behind 5 Second Networking is based solidly on the personal development principles of clarity and focus.

You want to become a "Mental Billboard" at a networking meeting by delivering you single most important and unique value in less than 5 seconds. What is it that you do best and most profitably?   Focus exclusively on that and nothing else. When you do – you increase the likelihood that your listening audience will as well, that your impression will be lasting and positive.

In 5 seconds tell me how you want to be remembered.

People are like rope.

~

When you put them under a strain
they can do a lot of creaking and groaning...

Some are very flexible.
Some can be unbending
and harder to work with.

But you never know
how much they can really handle
until something snaps
&
things start to unravel...

Predictions are based principally on two factors
– Human Nature & Economic Necessity –
these are merely logical projections based on known conditions

Green Energy

The need for alternative forms of clean, renewable energy in the US will be driven by three factors.

1. Demand – The US consumes 20% of the world's energy and as existing resources are depleted, or diverted to other emerging economies availability goes down and prices go up. It is that simple.
2. Deficit – A large percentage of our looming net negative trade imbalance is due directly to petroleum imports. Reducing our dependency on that improves our import/export ratios and helps control debt.
3. Employment – lower, controllable cost energy along with the technology and production of the means to generate that energy means more jobs.

It would be nice I suppose if the driving head behind our development of environmentally sound, renewable energy sources were altruistic but it is not. If it were, more would have been done along these lines over the past forty years. America's push to regain energy independence will be powered by economic survival and the demands of her people – which is why it will have traction.

Opportunity will present itself first in power conservation and savings systems and methods followed by alternative generation and transmission/distribution solutions.

PERSON "A"	PERSON "B"
Cheerful	Morose
Trustworthy	Sneaky
Hard working	Lazy
Positive	Complainer
Genuine	Self-important
Team player	Selfish
Focused	Disinterested
Kind	Gossip
Pleasant	Mean spirited
Flexible	Rigid
Enthusiastic	Indifferent
On time	Late or absent
Careful	Sloppy
Motivated	No initiative
Avid learner	Resists change
Cooperative	Out for himself
Communicator	Loner
Creative vision	Linear thinker

There are two candidates for a job with virtually identical resumes. They have basically the same educational background and work experience. They are looking for the same compensation.

Which one would you rather hire?

If both of these people worked for you and you had to fire one, who would go and who would stay?

The answer is pretty obvious in both cases. However there is something very important to remember about human nature and business. When it happens to somebody else, it is just business. When it happens to us, it is personal.

Keeping that in mind – where do you fit in these columns and what do you think you might want to improve, to improve your odds of success?

I am three people.

I am who I think I am,

I am who others think I am,
&
I am who I am.

(which usually resides somewhere between the first two)

A man in a diner says to the waitress "I'll have a cup of coffee without cream, please."

The waitress comes back a few minutes later and says "I'm sorry, but we're all out of cream. Would you mind taking your coffee without milk?"

***

When we focus on the wrong things we waste time, court argument and ultimately failure. Simply because something is factual doesn't make it relevant. Yet it is our nature to form our point of view and look for things that support our decisions rather than those things which may contradict them. As a result we may not give the appropriate weight to other opinions, to our detriment.

When we embrace the fact that we can be wrong without succumbing to self-doubt; we become more open-minded, we encourage others to share their opinions and we recognize the difference between constructive and destructive criticism (putting each where it belongs). As a result we get better and more complete outcomes.

Take it a step further. How often do we argue with people we already share a common goal with? Both parties want the same thing (in this case – black coffee), why not start there. If we cannot find a way to synthesize success with our friends and allies – how can we hope to convince others with different viewpoints to share our vision?

WOULD YOU:

...follow someone that doesn't believe in what they are doing?

...follow someone who doesn't know where they are going?

...invest in a company if the owners weren't willing to risk their own capital?

...willingly work long hours for someone who leaves early?

...promise something you can't deliver just to get rid of someone annoying?

...work at a job you hate?

...sell a product or service that you wouldn't buy?

...tell your boss off if you could?

...have respect for people who do not respect you?

..rather go through the motions, not make waves?

...change something if you could?

In a world fueled by technological expansion, it is universally agreed that the future belongs to the well educated… AND it is also agreed that our educational system is broken. Bad combination.

Rather than open a discussion of "how to fix our schools" I would rather go a level deeper and examine what an educated person must look like in a world in which the knowledge base changes almost by the minute.

Knowledge no longer has intrinsic value.

The ability to see patterns, trends, how things interact and interconnect has value. The ability to solve problems, think laterally, to make the creative leap and find synergy has value. It is not about "knowing"… it is about knowing where to find it and how to apply it that has value.

The two most important things one can do for such a world is to "learn how to learn" quickly, efficiently… and how to "un-learn". We must learn how to discard outdated notions or they will hold you back.

One of the greatest dangers of such a world is that technology attempts to make experience obsolete by enabling people to perform complex tasks without a learning curve BUT then we don't learn anything. Technology cannot replace experience; it is an imposter but complacency embraces it because it is easy and expedient. In fact, when we rely on such a path we sacrifice the development of critical problem solving and diagnostic skills. We start to lose the ability to see how pathways combine and interrelate because such a system focuses only on outcomes.

What this does is create a divide, a disparity where the majority of people "know the answer is 42" because "42 is what it says when I push these buttons".

In creating a "black box" disposable society *we forgot that we are society and risk becoming disposable ourselves…*

In 1860, Abe Lee struck gold in Leadville Colorado.

The town had been aptly named for the huge quantities of lead carbonite that seemed to be everywhere.

The resulting gold strike petered out relatively quickly and of course the miners followed news of the next strike.

But they had missed something...

The massive amounts of lead carbonite contained silver, large percentages of silver and just a few years later in the mid 1870's the town had produced millionaires such as Horace and Baby Doe Tabor as well as JJ and the "Unsinkable" Molly Brown.

At the height of production the Matchless Mine alone produced over $2000 per day of high grade silver and more than $7 million over its lifetime. This was at a point in history when the average American worker labored for about a dollar a day.

The silver had always been there but people ignored it because they were focused on something else.

Now isn't that just like an opportunity – hiding in plain sight.

"You should be ashamed," the father told his son, "When Abraham Lincoln was your age, he used to walk ten miles every day to school."

"Really?" the kid said. "When he was your age, he was president."

***

It is easy to find fault with others. More often than not it will make them resentful. Even if well-intentioned, human nature tends to see criticism more as a weapon than a tool. Unfortunately because that is how so many people use it.

Once said, nothing can ever truly be rescinded.
No apology, however sincere can ever reset the clock.

If your words have teeth when they leave-
they will have grown fangs by the time they return.

Man is a social creature by nature. That is why we formed tribes and clans. That is why we built towns and cities. That is the driving force behind the social networking phenomena today. It is in our DNA. It kept us alive when much stronger, faster things with larger, sharper teeth wanted to eat us.

We are hardwired to both compete and cooperate. They are both just tools but we function most efficiently through collaboration because it finds ways where everyone contributes and benefits. However competition has become the rule of the day. The problem with that is that in order for one to win, everyone else must lose. What is the purpose of Wall Street if not to keep score? Would professional athletes command the salaries they do, would fans spend billions on team paraphernalia, tickets and souvenirs if no one kept score? If no one lost, would companies line up to pay for advertising time and endorsements?

Probably not. Yet what are teams, companies, organizations, cities, even entire countries and cultures if not cooperative models, within themselves?

It is only against "the outsider" that we compete.

In the course of societal evolution, as mankind got better at the survival of their group they would turn their attention to their next proximate threat. As individual tribes grew stronger (through internal cooperation) their next most powerful threat became the "tribe next door". Competition grew.

With the increase of towns and cities came an increased division of labor, a class system and economic competition. Broadening commerce and trade meant man needed a way to "keep score" – money entered the scene and competition increased yet again.

The point is that as individual organisms we compete against each other but as soon as we are formed into groups - cooperation makes us stronger, smarter and more efficient.

Given the shrinking nature of the world, the explosion of population and diminishing resources; cooperation is more critical than ever and competition which seeks to increase the distance and disparity between people only compounds instability in an already dangerous world.

What does it profit a person, company or country for that matter to be the strongest branch on a dead tree?   The problem with living in a vacuum is that it is so very hard to breath.

Children's stories are fascinating…

Take for example the story of the **Tortoise and the Hare**.

The moral is "Slow and steady wins the race".

BUT does it really?

The hare was infinitely better suited to run the race than his adversary however his over confidence and resulting lack of focus caused him to lose <u>one</u> race. The tortoise didn't win. He merely crossed the finish line first. He had one successful result but he didn't become any faster. He didn't improve or evolve. The tortoise is the champion, but it is a non-sustainable position.

What are the chances that the hare might lose in a rematch or a hundred rematches for that matter? If the hare walks away resolved to never let his ego get the better of him again and remain focused on his goals as a result of this rather embarrassing defeat – isn't he the real winner?

It is the hare, not the tortoise that has an opportunity to gain from this outcome.

Maybe the moral should be; focus.
  Or perhaps, winning and losing are relative.

Thomas Jefferson said,
"The harder I work, the luckier I get."

Luck is a crumb that drops from opportunity's table...

instead of hoping one falls
wouldn't you rather
pull up a chair
and fill your plate?

(Oh, that's where the"hard work" part comes in)

Two people are at a resort.
The first turns to this friend and says, "The food here is just awful.
I can barely choke it down."

The friend replies, "I know, and such small portions."

***

We find what we look for. Abraham Lincoln said, "If you look for the evil in a man, you'll find it." So why bother to point fingers and find fault – unless it is to learn from it and fix it...

If we want positive outcomes (AKA opportunity) – isn't that what we should be looking for? Don't worry, there will be plenty of other people to wallow in misery, they won't miss you if you leave.

The Myth of MORE than ENOUGH

We only need enough.

but society tries to convince us we need more than enough...

but you can never have more than enough,

by definition because there is always something more....

something else that's shiny, newer, faster...

It leaves us feeling forever dissatisfied

spiritually and financially bankrupt.

Remember when you define what success looks like –
be very careful what yardstick you use to measure it by...
Beware the Myth of MORE than ENOUGH.

During the dark days of the Civil War, Abraham Lincoln's Secretary of War, a man named Stanton chastised the president, "Why do you spend so much time trying to befriend your enemies when you should be destroying them?"

Lincoln replied, "If I turn an enemy into a friend – haven't I destroyed that enemy?"

What people often fail to grasp is the Myth of Friends and Enemies.

We often make the mistake of thinking just because something is powerful it is a threat. Why couldn't it just as easily be a potent ally?

Look at technology – it can be something as simple as fire or as complex as nuclear power. Fire can heat a home or burn it to the ground. I can use the energy of the atom to light a city or level it. Same energy – same technology – different choices.

Resources such as power and wealth possess no will of their own. We impose our will to bend it to our ends. They are neither friend nor foe until we make them into one or the other. When we hold back it is because we fear our own abilities. If you wish to accomplish great things, at some point you must take hold of and control power. There is no option, except to wait and delay. Why would you want to do that?

In a competitive world, strength represents a potential threat, a danger.

In a cooperative world, strength is courted as a potential ally.

The greatest example of this is shown on the following page:

The single greatest motivator of the human animal is FEAR.

It is not an emotion, it is a physiological response. That is why your heart races, your palms sweat and you get a knot in the pit of your stomach... Fight or Flight – it is hardwired into us.

-    **FEAR CAN BE YOUR MOST POWERFUL FRIEND OR ENEMY**   -

When FEAR stands before us it holds us back...

When we put FEAR behind us it drives us forward.

This is the part that is really cool –

You get to choose...

A man and his wife went to the state fair every year. One of the attractions was a ride in an old fashioned bi-plane like they used in WWI. Every year the husband would say, "Boy, I'd like to ride in that airplane." And every year his wife would say, "You always say that, but that ride costs ten dollars, and ten dollars is ten dollars."

Finally one year they at the fair the man said, "I'm 81 years old. If I don't ride that airplane this year I may never get another chance."

His wife replied, "Well, that airplane ride costs ten dollars, and ten dollars is ten dollars."

The pilot overheard them and said, "Folks, I'll make you a deal. I'll take you both up for a ride. If you can stay quiet for the entire trip and not say one word, I won't charge you, but if you say one word you pay full fare."

They agreed and climbed into the open cockpit. The pilot did all kinds of twists and turns, rolls and dives, without a peep from his passengers. He repeated all his tricks over again, but still not a word.

They landed and the pilot turned to the man, "I did everything I could think of to get you to yell out, but you didn't."

The man replied, "Well, you almost had me when Eloise fell out on that last big loop d 'loop, but ten dollars is ten dollars."

***

This is an amazingly complex story about goals, dreams, frustration and priorities (of the misplaced variety). It begs the questions of "What would you do if money were no object?" and "What would you tolerate if money were the only object?"

Wow…

Stress and fear are integrally linked. Each one catalyzes the other.

We worry about our jobs, our families, our mortgage, our retirement, what the neighbors will think, what the out come of the next election will be, eColi in hamburger and who will win the big game...

Wait a minute. Does all that angst alter the outcome? The only thing worry and stress changes is us (and not for the better).

Moreover, stress is contagious. It is a social disease. We pick it up from people around us and then infect others.

Everything in your life can be placed in one of three categories:

1. Things you have control over like your personal space, your attitude, how you react to things.
2. Things you can influence, like family, friends and co-workers.
3. Things over which you have no control, like the weather, tidal surges, volcanic eruptions and the movement of celestial bodies.

Stress is a lifestyle choice. So is it's absence...

In the first case it only hurts me. Since these are things over which I exert direct control. Stress is caused by concern over the outcome of decisions I have made or will make... if I am stressed I must not have much faith in my own ability to make good choices. If I am confident in my decision making capability – why would I be stressed. Remember the famous words of President Harry Truman, "When in doubt, I make a decision. If I'm wrong, I'll make another."

In the second case, when we work toward reducing stress for those around us – don't we also reduce it for ourselves (remember – it's a social disease).

In the third case, how we react to situations over which we have no control will not alter the condition, but it does alter us and isn't it always preferable that our choices move us in a positive direction?

FDR said, "We have nothing to fear but fear itself." Fear itself *is* stress.

> "We are what we repeatedly do. Excellence, then, is not an act, but a habit..."
>
> Aristotle

When we develop good habits *they serve us...*

When we develop bad habits *we serve them...*

That's the funny thing about habits, they make wonderful servants and terrible masters.

To succeed you must persevere...
To persevere – you must exercise self discipline.
Self discipline works best when it becomes habit.

Why did the chicken cross the road?

Answer: To get to the other side

***

How could this possibly be relevant?

Sometimes the answer is just the answer.
Avoid the temptation to "over-analyze" things. It can paralyze you.

The first of three qualities of success that rise above all others.

CLARITY

If I cannot clearly, succinctly, specifically define my goals – I am navigating blind. I often ask people what they need next in their business and find they can't tell me. They either don't know or cannot precisely say what it is and why they need it. How can someone help you get what you need if even you don't know what it is? I will ask them to describe their most profitable customer and they don't know what that person looks like. How can you hope to find them and clone them if you don't have clear picture of what they look like?

Clarity begins by asking yourself challenging questions like:

> Don't tell me what you make or what service you provide –
> What problem do you solve?

> Don't tell me you need more customers -
> Tell me who has that problem?

> Don't tell me you need money –
> How much?
> Why that amount?
> What you will use it for?

Everything must happen in its proper order. You can't fix the roof, until you fix the hammer...

> What impediments or steps stand between you and the goal?
> In what order?
> What do you need to set them right?

Solid, efficient outcomes happen faster and more profitably with clarity.

The second of three qualities of success that rise above all others.

<u>FOCUS</u>

Once you have a clear picture of your objective, you need make it centric to all your activity.

We live in the information age and it is that overload which conspires to divert and redirect our attention. How many times during the course of an average day do we shift gears mentally? We are confronted with a multitude of tasks often overlapping. In light of this competition for our attention, how easy is it to become distracted?

In text, graphic, a recording, create an icon of your goal. Make it as real and as tactile as possible and revisit it often, several times a day to keep it forefront in your thoughts.

The third of three qualities of success that rise above all others.

<u>PERSISTENCE</u>

Failure is a choice. Success is a process built of habit.

A marathon is over 26 miles long but it is only the very last step that actually determines the winner. There is nothing that fuels success more than sheer dogged determination, the refusal to settle for less.

The formula is simple. Find it, fix it in your mind and let nothing deter you.

The rest is incidental

Predictions are based principally on two factors
– Human Nature & Economic Necessity –
these are merely logical projections based on known conditions

The Aging Problem

The graying of America, coupled with the decline and uncertainty of funds available for retirement will result in a large step "backward" in the makeup of society. This will be further exacerbated by the economic necessity of multiple income family units due to the rising cost of higher education, healthcare and the cost of care for minor children.

The shift I am referring to is a growing return to the multi-generational household. Much of the world has never departed from this model. It has a proven track record as the most successful and efficient means for sustaining a stable environment since the dawn of civilization. Just as they have for centuries seniors would provide domestic help, child care and economic assistance and in return they would be able to live at a comfortable level they could otherwise not afford. Everyone wins.

In addition by providing effectively one on one child rearing and nurturing, young children would be better positioned for success educationally.

The sandwich generation will in essence become; an open faced sandwich.

Economically this will directly affect the need for services like stand alone day care and assisted living facilities – however recall the empire Martha Stewart built. She recognized that America's latchkey generations lacked basic domestic skills and in making them available she positioned herself to make a fortune. Nature abhors a vacuum. Nothing changes without an equivalent opportunity rushing in.

The Myth of Obsolete

In technology, we often hear that this or that is "Obsolete".

But is it? Simply because there is a newer version that has been introduced?

In soft economic conditions, people "make do" and that means opportunity. Very lucrative niche businesses have grown up quite successfully serving the needs of customers who possess and use "obsolete stuff".

For example; in the mailing machine industry - between 1920 and 1980 equipment had become increasingly sophisticated with the addition of electronics. The basic mechanics of opening an envelope, inserting folded letters / bills / notices then sealing, stamping and addressing them had not really changed much. A company on Long Island, NY realized this and made a simple clone of a 1920's era machine which sold for a fraction of the price charged by their state of the art competitors. They never intended to satisfy everyone, simply that segment of the market which needed an "obsolete" no frills machine. It was a very successful strategy.

Consider human nature (which inherently resists change). Assume 15% of the marketplace are "early adaptors" and 10% will never change. That means in your field 75% of the market may continue to use something "obsolete" until they get around to integrating the "new" version or model.

What the innovator often does is not just made their old product obsolete... they may make a lot of their customers obsolete.

Change *always* brings opportunity.

**nothing you can do
alters your past**

~

**everything you do
determines
your future...**

Self Improvement is like the Lottery.

Assume that to win a lottery you need to select 6 numbers in the right order from an initial pool of 50.

The odds of winning are over 11 Billion to 1.

You can choose to simply buy a ticket and accept the odds, but your chances are really not very good.

What if you knew for a certainty what 2 of the numbers would be?

Now your odds of winning improve to just over 5.5 Million to 1.
(That's 2000 times better)

Now suppose that you knew what 4 of the numbers would be?

Your odds of winning would be 1 out of 2450.

That's a world of difference.

~

As we take charge of our lives
as we build our character and attitude around a more successful paradigm,
as we cultivate the habits of successful people,
we continually improve our odds of winning.

Or you can choose to simply buy a ticket and wait...
and hope...

Children's stories are fascinating...

Let's look at **The Wolf in Sheep's Clothing** -

It has taken a lot of different forms and twists but the upshot is always the same. Evil intentions can be hidden behind a harmless or appealing veneer.

Sooner or later, what you do speaks louder than anything you could say.

In the Law of Association we are drawn to those who share our value systems. That is not to say that there are people who will pose as something they are not to "sneak through the transom". There will always be those eager to harvest the low hanging fruit and run off – but they usually show themselves quickly.

This is why the Law of Association works best and most powerfully in the cooperative model, because we look out for each other's interests.

If the sheep were to adopt a "better him than me" attitude, it would not be long before the flock was decimated. It is not merely a question of strength in numbers. It is about the creation of group through a shared interest, common objectives, and like-minded purpose. That is the Law of Association in action.

Everyday a man was verbally and psychologically abused by his boss.
He was continually subjected to a never-ending barrage of insults.
"How can you be so stupid?"
"You know better.
"What the heck is the matter with you?"
It got to the point where he just seemed to dread his days.
After all, the outcome was inevitable.
No matter how much he did right, his boss was right there to hound him with every mistake he had ever made.
He tried to convince himself it didn't matter, but it didn't do any good.
If he slacked off, he heard about it instantly.
His life was miserable but what could he do –
He was self-employed...

Regardless of whether you are a volunteer or work for a paycheck - whether you are salaried or commissioned – whether you are an "underling" or "the Big Boss" we are all self-employed. *(And we are often our own harshest critics)*

Positive feedback is intended to help us improve. Negative feedback dooms us to making the same mistakes again and again. There is only one thing that determines whether feedback is positive or negative and that is how you choose to receive it. Even though it may be well-intentioned; constructive comments may still be viewed negatively and even the harshest criticism may be accepted and turned to positive action by the recipient. I cannot alter "your intent" but I can control my reaction.

Ultimately – it is not the critic, but the one chastised who determines the result. It is the attitude of the person on the receiving end that sees the comments as merely hurtful, or seeks to make it an opportunity for growth.

Empowered "self-employed" people choose the latter.

A few tips on How to run a Successful 5 Second Networking Meeting.

One of the biggest distractions at a networking meeting is the notion that "I need to get everyone's card". Take that off the table by collecting a business card from each attendee and tell everyone that a scanned copy of every card will be emailed to every person present. If they do not have their email on their card, ask them to write it on the reverse of their card. Have blank cards available if someone forgot their cards. If they do not supply a valid email – they cannot enjoy the benefit.

Everyone must agree to a ZERO TOLERANCE spamming policy.

What this does is free the "stress load" of "I might not get their card…" People don't have to worry about running out of cards, or losing them. It sets a better tone and permits everyone to relax a little.

Always set the ground rules:

1. Criticism is a gift – it should always be intended to hone and improve one another and it should be accepted in that spirit.
2. Never deviate from 5 seconds. No questions or comments from the floor. That is what networking time is for.
3. Avoid the temptation to "sell" – simply state what you do best and most profitably. Let it stand on its own, a mental billboard.
4. There are no guarantees to get or give referrals. The pressure to do that often backfires. If you know of a legitimate need for another's product or service, tell them If you know someone else who might be a resource – put them in touch.

You should always have at least four 5 second responses in mind.

What your company does best and most profitably (the pitch). What your most profitable client looks like (your prospect). What you need next in your business (your immediate goal). What your end game is (your ultimate goal). You should know all four of these like your middle name

In Robert Frost's poem, <u>Mending Wall</u> – the poet says," Before I build a wall I like to ask what I am walling out and walling in".

In networking and building our strategic resource alliances, we can go deep or we can go broad. Look at the Venn diagrams below. When we only network concentrically inward using groups to wall each other off – we get very strong alliances but less exposure to new ideas and influences. When we spread ourselves too thin we may get lots of new ideas, in fact at times too many that can cloud our vision.

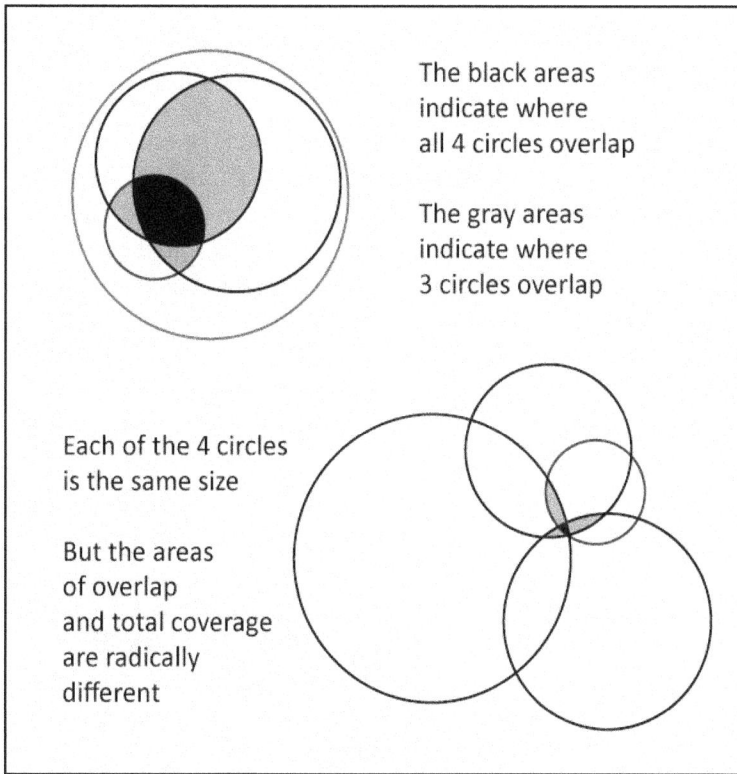

The black areas indicate where all 4 circles overlap

The gray areas indicate where 3 circles overlap

Each of the 4 circles is the same size

But the areas of overlap and total coverage are radically different

We need depth and breadth. We need balance but our core principles are the litmus test to tell us when we are reaching too far.

A Story -

A father saw his young son looking very dejected. "Why so sad?" he asked. "They tested everybody in gym today to see how high they could jump and everyone was better than me... and in two weeks they are going to test everybody again. It was embarrassing." he replied.

The father thought a minute and said, "Well I think we can do something about that." He had the boy jump as high as he could next to the wall. Then he put a piece of masking tape where his outstretched hand had touched to mark the spot. "Now then," the father said, "every day I want you to practice jumping up and touching that spot. I think pretty soon we'll see a difference."

Everyday the boy diligently jumped to touch the tape again and again. The day before he was to be re-tested, the boy said to his father, "Tomorrow we get tested and I still can barely reach the tape. I haven't gotten any better." The father looked at him and said, "Never mind that. Tomorrow you just jump as high as you can. I believe in you. You have been working hard to improve and I think that you might just surprise yourself."

***

The next day the excited boy ran to his father and announced that he had jumped higher than everyone else... "But I don't understand how..." he said.

The father smiled, "I do. You see every night when you went to sleep – I moved the tape up a little bit. I knew you could jump higher but you had to overcome something much tougher than just gravity. You had to get over doubting yourself. People often have more in them than they give themselves credit for. You just needed to see that for yourself. So next time you have to jump high don't be afraid, just let 'er rip."

Moral – *We make the lines, we can move them.*
When we move the line to make it easier, we accept limitations.
We grow when we move the line to stretch our limits.

The Admiral on the bridge of his flagship steamed full speed ahead through a thick fog bank. Just ahead he saw the lights of another ship and had his radioman send out a message.

"Turn 5 degrees starboard"

A moment later the reply came, "No – you turn 5 degrees port"

Furious the Admiral wired back,

"This is a battleship – turn 5 degrees starboard immediately"

Then came the reply, "This is a lighthouse. If I were you I'd turn 5 degrees port and I'd hurry."

***

We tend to assume that our reality is the reality for everyone else. Not so. Everyone has their own set of circumstances, ideals, dreams, fears and goals. Opportunity often rests where those pathways intersect.

One of the best ways to achieve our own objectives is to help others achieve theirs by running a parallel path.

It is the model of cooperation in action, helping each other succeed.

The Myth of Winning and Losing

We think of winning and losing as places. We even say "He came in first place" or "He came in last place". But if you "win" you do not get to stay there forever. There will always be another challenge and another challenger.

Winning and losing are at best only temporary conditions that someone with a scorecard and a clock artificially imposes.

It is not the result that makes us stronger or weaker – faster or slower, it is the contest itself.

The enlightened and empowered person understands that regardless of any one outcome, regardless of whether they "win or lose", they can never be beaten. They recognize that all of it is just an opportunity to grow stronger.

A Paradox

It is said <u>Misery Loves Company</u>.

What I cannot understand is when so many people might choose to embrace misery in their lives; that being said - misery must have all the company it could hope for.

If misery has all the company it could hope for; misery must be surrounded by everyone it loves. Misery should be ecstatic, delighted, happy beyond belief...

So why is misery so miserable?
I guess we need to be careful what we wish for.

The world's greatest chess player is challenged to a best out of three matches by a complete unknown, yet the challenger wins...
How is that possible? (answer below)

What automation "does" is to perform repetitive tasks quickly and precisely without getting tired, hungry or stressed.

What automation "does not" do is display things like:

> **Initiative** – the most sophisticated robot can't turn itself on. It can't decide to study something on its own.
>
> **Ambition** - the most sophisticated robot can't decide to work harder or put in a few more hours to better itself.
>
> **Creativity** - the most sophisticated robot can't synthesize a better solution from seemingly unconnected ideas.
>
> **Leadership** - the most sophisticated robot can't rally the other robots by setting a good example.

The most sophisticated robot can't brain storm with the other robots. it can't exhibit curiosity, compassion, management ability, people skills or enthusiasm...

The most sophisticated robot can't make itself indispensible through its decisions and actions.

The only way you can lose your job to a robot is if you are doing the job of a robot, like a robot. You are playing their game by their rules. If that is the case you will lose. If that is the case, change the game. By the way – that is what our challenger above did. He and the chess master played golf.

In this

crazy, TOPSY TURVY, stressed out

world

***

You cannot grab

anything

until

you

let

go

of

something

else

FIRST!

The Myth of Perfection

If perfection could be achieved – it would be static.

Any movement or change from that position would be by definition "something other than perfect".

So if perfection could exist here, it would at best be only for a moment and vanish unless we take a different view of it.

As people, our greatest value is found not in achieving perfection but in pursuing it. It is to strive to be the best that we can be from moment to moment. Unfortunately in that pursuit we often find ourselves discouraged.

Consider this analogy:

A barrel full of rocks sits beside the ocean.
It cannot hold the ocean; that is impossible.
But it can hold a barrel full of "something".

The person who is not empowered shrugs their shoulders and walks away accepting the barrel as is.

The empowered person, knowing there is still room in the barrel - fills it to the brim with as much of the ocean as it can hold.

The enlightened person starts taking the rocks out.

The barrel will never hold the ocean – but it can hold all it can hold.
Our lives are like those barrels – how will you choose to fill yours?

Children's stories are fascinating...

How about **Rumplestiltskin** -

He was the little gnome who spun straw into gold.

A young peasant girl's father bragged that his daughter was so smart she could spin straw into gold until news of it reaches the King. (Sound familiar, other people making promises that you have to deliver on.)

The King imprisons and threatens the girl unless she spins rooms full of straw into gold. (He really needs to rethink his management style.)

Twice the gnome helps her out for a small fee. The third time she has nothing left to pay him and agrees to give him her first born child. (She sacrifices a possible future event for an immediate need – not uncommon and often not a great deal.)

After the third time around the King is so overjoyed (he is also both incredibly wealthy and out of straw) he marries the girl. (I wonder if that is love or fear of loss working in the relationship...)

Naturally they have a child and Rumplestiltskin comes to collect the debt. The Queen is so distraught that the gnome agrees to release her from her promise if she can guess his name within three days. The Queen uses her power and position to spy on him and discover his true identity. (I guess she learned a lot from the King). At any rate the little gnome is forced to vanish angrily and empty handed.

The moral: When you can put a name and a face to your fear it becomes manageable and goes away. But I still think the little guy got short changed (no pun intended) and all things considered, the kid might have been better off with him.

We are hardwired for both
COOPERATION
&
COMPETITION

They are just tools.
Successful people know how and when to use both.
You don't use a hammer to drive screws.

Cooperation
needs to be *external*
building
Strategic Resource Alliances.
(The Law of Association)

Competition
needs to be *internal*
spurring us to constantly improve ourselves.

Our most difficult obstacles are the ones we put in front of ourselves.

Competing internally strengthens us while moving these things out of our way. It makes us a more attractive target for potential strategic collaboration because our strength attracts more strength as a peer. But if we compete with others it only strengthens them to oppose us.

The broader our array of resources, the more we encourage others to join in the more we have to draw on BUT people will often reject networking because they want to restrict their association only to those people who can aid them. That is the wolf in sheep's clothing. It is competition masquerading as cooperation. To get help we must give help – remember we pour water into the top of a glass but it fills from the bottom up.

If your mind is closed...

How is opportunity going to get in?

If the oddly disconnected manner in which this book is written frustrates and annoys you, that's good.

The way in which we communicate has evolved – we too must evolve or perish. That is basic biology.

Back in the 1970's a reporter asked the author Kurt Vonnegut why the chapters in his novels were so short. He replied that he wrote them so that the average person could read one in ten minutes, the time between television commercials because that had become the attention span of the American people.

To see the reason why I chose to write this book in this fashion you need look no further than the television remote (if you can find it). Watch how people watch television, they constantly leap between channels and rewind the DVR.

Consider for a moment the phenomena of new media such as blogging, RSS feeds, Twitter, texting… communication has evolved into micro-bursts.

Gleaning information has become the synthesis of super compressed bytes of data scattered in multiple formats. It is all about the ability to associate effectively, but our nature fearing the poverty of time in our lives will usually freeze us in place or cause us to leap prematurely.

To be successful today you must stand at the crossroads of that synthesis firmly rooted in an awareness of our own nature while maintaining an open attitude toward growth and opportunity. You must plug into strategic alignments to parlay our abilities through cooperative networking alliances. We can never stop learning, unlearning and relearning. Or you could simply change the channel.

Good Luck (but of course – you make your own luck.)

www.ingramcontent.com/pod-product-compliance
Lightning Source LLC
Chambersburg PA
CBHW060631210326
41520CB00010B/1556